Accelerated Learning

How to Learn Fast: Effective Advanced Learning Techniques to Improve Your Memory, Save Time and Be More Productive

Kevin Garnett

© **Copyright 2020** by Kevin Garnett – All rights reserved.

In no way is it legal to reproduce, duplicate, or transmit any part of this document in either electronic means or in printed format. Recording of this publication is strictly prohibited and any storage of this document is not allowed unless with written permission from the publisher.

The information provided herein is stated to be truthful and consistent, in that any liability, in terms of inattention or otherwise, by any usage or abuse of any policies, processes, or directions contained within is the solitary and utter responsibility of the recipient reader. Under no circumstances will any legal responsibility or blame be held against the author for any reparation, damages, or monetary loss due to the information herein, either directly or indirectly.

The information herein is offered for informational purposes solely, and is universal as so. The presentation of the information is without contract or any type of guarantee assurance.

Medical Disclaimer: This book does not contain any medical advice. The ideas and suggestions contained in this book are not intended as a substitute for consulting with your doctor. All matters regarding your health require medical supervision.

Legal Disclaimer: all photos used in this book are licensed for commercial use or in the public domain.

ERRORS

Please contact me if you find any errors.

My publisher and I have taken every effort to ensure the quality and correctness of this book. However, after going over the book draft time and again, we sometimes don't see the forest for the trees anymore.

If you notice any errors, I would really appreciate it if you could contact me directly before taking any other action. This allows me to quickly fix it.

Errors: errors@semsoli.com

REVIEWS

Reviews and feedback help improve this book and the author.

If you enjoy this book, I would greatly appreciate it if you were able to take a few moments to share your opinion and post a review online.

Table of Contents

Introduction	9
Chapter 1: What is Accelerated Learning?	13
The Basic Principles	15
Holistic Approach	16
Chapter 2: The Origin of Accelerated Learning	21
Before Accelerated Learning was a Thing...	21
Bridging the Achievement Gap	24
Chapter 3: Your Brain is Malleable, Your Intelligence Is Not Fixed	29
What is the Value of an IQ Test score?	30
Growth Mindset vs Fixed Mindset	32
What is Your Mindset?	37
Chapter 4: Let's Get Practical! Four Simple Techniques To Learn Faster	39
Mind Mapping	39
Chunking	40
Link Items With Places and Images	41
Do the Opposite of What You are Doing That's Not Working	43
Chapter 5: How to Create A Positive Working And Learning Environment	45
Create A Stimulating Environment	47

Establish an Atmosphere Where Failure Is Fine	50
The Secret to Achieving Your Goals: Enjoyment	53
A Positive Environment Is A Safe Environment	57

Chapter 6: The Trick to Learning Like a Pro — 65

Traditional Learning is Boring	66
Visual Aids Help, But...	67
The Trick: Get Active!	68
Feedback	71

Chapter 7: Different Learning Styles And How You Can Use Them — 75

Visual Learners	76
Aural Learners	77
Physical Learners	78
Verbal Learners	81
Logical Learners	82
Social Or Solitary Learning	84

Chapter 8: Accelerated Learning and the Importance of Context — 87

Symbol Process Learning	88
Symbol Process Learning – Not For Everyone	90
Accelerated Learning in Context	91

Chapter 9: Metacognition – The Key To Effective Accelerated Learning — 95

Metacognitive Learning	97

Chapter 10: More Practical Tips for Accelerating Your Own Learning — 103

Teaching Others Teaches Yourself	103

Question	104
Have A Conversation…With Yourself	104
Get Out the Colored Crayons	105
Keep Motivated	106
If You Can't Do, Think	107
Move	108
Final Words	**109**
Resources	**111**
BONUS CHAPTER: What is Stoicism	**113**
What is Stoicism?	114
The Origin of Stoicism	117
The Most Important Stoic Philosophers	120
Did You Like This Book?	**125**

Introduction

When did you learn best?

Perhaps your response is: in elementary school. Or maybe you think it was in college.

But you'd be wrong. You learned best *when you were a young child*, before you even went to school! As a child, you didn't focus on learning itself. Instead, you learned by doing. By copying what you saw around you, through trial and error.

My little nephew is just learning to walk, which is a perfect illustration of what I mean. By now, he has learned how to stand. But he is still afraid of walking without support. But he's at the point where he wants to learn. When he stands, and I'm close to him, he'll stick out his hands to me for support, and then we walk together. Or he walks behind a little car, which he can also use for support. He's falling and getting up all the time.

But he's not afraid to fail. And, more importantly, he's enjoying it!

How does that compare to studying for an exam in high school? Or struggling to come up with the right answer on your math test?

In school, many of us develop negative associations with learning. So, when we finally have our degree, it's so easy to stop learning and avoid any real challenges.

However, if you want to live a fulfilled life, set goals and achieve them, understanding how you can learn effectively and with ease becomes a real asset!

This is where accelerated learning comes into play.

Accelerated learning is a set of simple techniques that you can incorporate into your daily life to improve your overall performance. By taking the challenges away, accelerated learning will make learning new things fun and exciting again!

It really works, and it offers opportunities for everybody, whether they have been successful in their education up to this point or found training and learning a challenge. By using accelerated learning techniques, you will learn better, faster, and with more understanding. And with understanding comes long term memory and recall.

After reading this book and applying the practices of accelerated learning, you will develop greater confidence, understand how to learn properly and effectively, and become more successful in achieving your goals, whatever they might be.

Imagine that you are studying for a promotion at work; you are worried, stressed, fearing that this could be your last chance. You spend hours reading and paraphrasing your notes. It is boring, tiring, and demoralizing.

By learning, understanding, and using accelerated reading techniques, you will become a better learner, you will be more successful in your endeavors, and this aspect of life will become a more positive experience for you. Follow the techniques and theories outlined in this book and those outcomes will be achieved.

So, I hope you are excited: let's get started with how you can use accelerated learning techniques to boost your productivity and become more successful!

Chapter 1: What is Accelerated Learning?

The problem from which you, I, and pretty much everybody else suffers is that education, whether for school, the workplace, or life in general, has shaped us. It has created prejudices, used largely unsuccessful methodology, and damaged the self-esteem of many. It has made us think of failure as a disaster. It has created the impression that we should get everything right – what are we learning if we can do it already? – and that to make mistakes or go through a learning process is somehow a bad thing. It has handicapped us with what Carol Dweck calls a 'fixed mindset'.

Accelerated learning is a way to overcome this. The concept of accelerated learning, sometimes simply called AL, is not a new one. However, its freshness of approach and its challenge to the traditional ways in which we learn new concepts and ideas makes it still a novel way to improve yourself.

In this chapter, we will look at some of the guiding principles behind accelerated learning, which come together to enable people to improve their understanding, problem solving, and acquisition of knowledge with remarkable effectiveness. The principles should be viewed rather like a recipe. Every element small or large plays an important role. Create the dish with just one ingredient missing and, while it won't kill you or send you rushing to the hospital with an acute case of food poisoning, it won't taste very good. Like a good cake, accelerated learning is all or nothing.

The Basic Principles

Underpinning the idea of accelerated learning are some basic, guiding principles.

Firstly, AL uses the idea of **exploiting and enhancing the ways in which people naturally learn**. This means that the system works as well with the four-year-old encountering letters for the first time as the eighty-year-old joining the University of Life and acquiring new skills for their later years.

The second underlying principle is that **accelerated learning seeks to break into the aspects of our potential which are often left undisturbed**, and therefore unused, by traditional teaching methods. It is common sense, if we think about it, that the more of our capabilities that are engaged by learning, the better we will learn. Therefore, this learning technique takes advantage of the numerous latent talents humans possess. It calls on the physical, creative, musical, artistic, visual, kinetic and emotional aspects of mankind, utilizing all of these in the development of the mind's learning capabilities.

Holistic Approach

Accelerated learning can best be described as a holistic approach to learning. As you head through this book you will come across tips to help you become an expert in this field. But, in a way, offering separate techniques is a little artificial. To become a proper, accelerated learner, you must apply the entire philosophy, rather than pick and choose only some of its elements.

This book will consider the following in more detail in later chapters, but accelerated learning makes sound assumptions about the way we learn and the environment which best enhances this.

- **The way we learn involves all of us**. For example, our brain processes information from each of the senses. Therefore, to maximize learning, we need to create the situation whereby the learner, be it ourselves or others, touches, smells, tastes, sees, and hears information.

- **Learners need to see their acquisition as creativity rather than consumption**. In traditional learning methods, the recipient is fed information or skills which they attempt to acquire. There are two fundamental failings with this approach. Firstly, learning is automatically limited by the range of the teaching material. Secondly, the brain is less effective at absorbing information than it is it at creating skills or knowledge, probably largely because being fed details is pretty boring, while being active and creative is more interesting.

- **Collaboration is a better way to learn than competition**. Of course, this is a concept which challenges the very heart of education, whether in the workplace, home, or educational institution. Examinations are competitive. Promotion at work is competitive. If we trace it back, we can see the reasons for this. Those expectations of a competitive environment are the product of people who were both themselves competitive and also successful in that competition. People recreate their own image. Yet it takes little thought to realize that competitive learning only suits those who are firstly competitive by their nature and secondly, successful at such competition. For the majority of people, in all walks of life, who simply are unmotivated by fighting against their peers, a competitive learning environment is one that is anathema to their naturally collaborative personalities.

- **People respond best to a variety of learning styles**. There can be a tendency on the part of the educator to attempt to replicate their own favored learning style as they impart their knowledge. As such, many people fail to be engaged as they are confronted with a style which counters their own.

- **When people learn, they do so on many different levels**. They can see things literally, metaphorically, intuitively, and so forth. They can acquire both practical skills and cognitive methods to problem solving; each has their place and is equally worthwhile. To illustrate the point with an example, in the traditional education system, cognitive abilities are frequently accorded higher status than practical ones, yet each plays their important role.

- **Learning is doing**. That is a key principle behind the theory of accelerated learning. It picks up on an earlier idea that when people are active, their ability to learn improves.

- **The brain is able to absorb information given in images instantly.**

- **The brain works better in a positive environment**. That does not mean, as is often interpreted, that everything in the environment is perfect, but more it means creating an environment in which learners, whatever their age of level, are confident and secure enough to feel able to test, experiment and, on occasion, fail. It is the ability to learn from that failure that encourages really deep and effective learning.

Next, we will look at the educational and social theory behind accelerated learning and discover a little of the history and context that underpins it.

Chapter 2: The Origin of Accelerated Learning

Back in the mid-1980s, the educational world was a very different place. There were enormous differences in achievement levels between different groups in society. Many would argue that this is still the case, but compared to thirty years ago, huge progress has been made.

Before Accelerated Learning was a Thing...

In those Reagan years, when the Cold War was coming towards its denouement and our view of the survival of the planet was still of secondary importance to driving big, flashy gas-guzzling cars and making loads of money, your culture, ethnicity, economic position and gender made even more of a difference towards your educational future than it does today. The bottom line hurts, but it still bears scrutiny. You were considerably more likely to be successful if you were middle class as opposed to working class, if you were white rather than black, if you were Christian rather than some other religion, if you were male rather than female.

Such inequality should be completely unacceptable in a civilized society, but those in power were the ones who belonged to the groups that did best, and so the urge for change was limited. Those who sought to bring about a fairer society were marginalized by the politics and media of white, middle class America.

This was not just a problem in the USA; indeed, across the developed Western world such inequality was rife.

In Australia, the last generation of Aboriginal children forcibly removed from their parents to be brought up by white families were reaching adulthood. This appalling breach of human rights had included mothers who could not read being told to sign forms which allowed a program of vaccination for their children, when in fact the form gave permission for their child to be adopted. At other times, officials simply took the children away. A country that views a significant portion of its population as sub-human cannot be expected to educate its citizens properly.

In the UK, the government of Margaret Thatcher – known in the educational world as "Thatcher, Thatcher, milk snatcher" for taking away school milk for primary-aged children during her time as Education Secretary – was removing investment from schools and creating a free market economy where greed was all. The "loadsamoney" culture, with white Yuppie types spending thousands on lunches and expensive champagne while homelessness and joblessness reached record highs, was dominant. At the same time, soccer stadium terraces were filled with fans performing racist chants and waving giant bananas at black players, and widespread violence was the norm.

Bridging the Achievement Gap

The system of accelerated learning was developed specifically to allow schools to challenge the achievement gap. Of course, today we can see how effectively the principles behind accelerated learning support all kinds of learning, not just for young people in schools, but back then it was developed as a social benefit which would challenge the status quo and raise achievement among all students.

The theory begins with the assumption that what we might call today "at-risk" students have gaps in their learning which lead, over time, to them falling further and further behind. Today we can see that it is not just at-risk students that have gaps in their learning, but that this applies to everybody, from the most disadvantaged kindergarten youngster to the most qualified and venerated of professors.

Addressing and closing those gaps allows people to make huge progress in their attainment of success. However, there have always been systems to help address gaps in learning. These remedial programs, though, were unsuccessful because they failed to use the strengths students already possessed, nor did they utilize the learning resources around them.

If a car has a hole in the underseal, then covering it with duct tape will not solve the problem; that tape will fall away quickly, perhaps even taking some of the rusting metal with it and creating bigger gaps. But use the surrounding strength of the remainder of the car's chassis and weld on a secure and permanent covering and that car is not only repaired, but stronger than it originally was.

Those early 1980s days were filled with optimism. In some ways that optimism was well deserved because progress has been made. In other ways, the utopia promised has failed to be delivered because there are vested interests in maintaining an achievement gap.

To become a successful institution to address the unfairness of the educational system back in the 1980s, schools needed to develop a unity of purpose. In other words, all stakeholders needed to buy into the priorities of the organization, not just its leaders, who would impose their values and beliefs on those lower down the totem pole. It can easily be seen how such an approach can apply equally well to a business as to a school. Power needs to be shared, with all members of the community put into a position to make decisions and see them through. Such procedures give empowerment to all stakeholders and removes the culture of blame and stagnation that can hit struggling organizations. Schools also needed to take stock of where they were and complete an audit of their strengths – and those of its extended community. Making use of such skills and resources that naturally existed, and using them to build on existing strengths leads to rapid and sustainable progress.

It is not just schools that can challenge this status quo, but we can as individuals, as well. If we buy into the concept of accelerated learning, if we stick to its principles and have faith in ourselves, we will become quicker and better learners. We will achieve more academically, both as individuals and – if our influence extends this far – also as institutions. Our workplaces, businesses, schools, and clubs will be more successful.

In the next chapters, we will look in more detail at these underlying principles upon which accelerated learning is founded.

Chapter 3: Your Brain is Malleable, Your Intelligence Is Not Fixed

What is your IQ?

Chances are, you've done an IQ test once. You got a certain score, and that's your IQ.

Right?

Wrong.

More and more scientific research is showing that our intelligence isn't fixed. From the field of epigenetics, to the work on fixed and growth mindsets by Carol Dweck, and the studies on the importance of deliberate practice by Anders Ericsson. They all point to the same thing: our brain – and thus our intelligence! – is malleable

What is the Value of an IQ Test score?

Not convinced yet?

Then let me tell you about the research done by James Flynn of the University of Otago, New Zealand. He demonstrated that in the years between 1947 and 2000, Americans gained:

- 24 points on IQ tests for similarities, while they only gained
- 4 points on vocabulary, and
- 2 points on math

An increase of 24 points in a little over 50 years! This isn't simply a genetic change, because there just isn't enough time for that to occur.

So how else can this be explained? And why is the increase so much more profound with regard to similarities as opposed to vocabulary and math?

The answer: we are using our intelligence in *different* ways now. We have more education now, more leisure activities. In the process, we have altered the balance between the abstract and concrete. Intelligence today involves the possibility to think outside the realm of personal observation and experience. And the good news: since the end of the study, access to online information has exploded. You can imagine that this develops our capabilities for similarities *even* further.

Seeing your intelligence as a fixed trait is a serious handicap if you want to apply accelerated learning techniques. As it turns out, changing your mindset is a real game-changer!

Growth Mindset vs Fixed Mindset

What's your first response to a challenge, something that is out of your comfort zone? Is your first impulse one of *"oh oh, I don't like this, I might fail at this."* Or does such a challenge excite you, because it is an opportunity for growth?

In her bestselling book, *Mindset: The Psychology of Success,* Carol Dweck - a professor in Psychology at Stanford University - found that two mindsets play an important role in all aspects of our lives:

- fixed mindset
- growth mindset

What's the difference between the two?

A **fixed mindset** is when people believe their basic qualities, their intelligence, their talents, their abilities, are just fixed traits. They have a certain amount, and that's that. On the other hand, people who have a **growth mindset** believe that even basic talents and abilities can be developed over time through experience, mentorship, and so on. And these are the people who go for it. They're not always worried about how smart they are, how they'll look, what a mistake will mean. They challenge themselves and grow.

Dweck became fascinated with intelligence when as a sixth-grader her teacher that year, Mrs. Wilson, seated her students around the room based on their IQ score. For her teacher, IQ her was the ultimate measure of your intelligence and your character.

Something similar happened to me when I was in the 8th and last year of elementary school. After doing an intelligence test, students were grouped together based on their performance. I was one of the 5 top-tier scores in a class of 25. I remember feeling weird about it, I didn't like being put on the spot like that. Also, I felt sorry for the students who were grouped together at the lowest-tier table. Surely that can't be good for the self-confidence of a 12-year old!

Contrary to what my teacher believed, Dweck's research has shown that our intelligence is not a fixed trait. Instead, it can be modified during one's lifetime.

In her experiment, she and her team had hundreds of students perform a test. Most of the students performed well on the test. After the test, they praised each student. But she used two different types of praise. Some were praised for their ability. They were told something along the lines of: *"Well done, you have a score of 85%. Really good.* **You must be very intelligent.***"*

Others were praised for their efforts. They were told: *"Well done, you have a score of 85%. Really good.* **You must have worked really hard.***"*

The first type of praise encourages a fixed mindset: that person was praised for a trait. The second type of praise encourages a growth mindset: that person was praised for his work, his efforts.

Then, the students were asked if they wanted to do challenging new task.
Many students who had received praise for their ability rejected the new task. They didn't want to do anything that could expose their flaws and call into question their talent.

In contrast, 90 percent of the students who were praised for their effort wanted the challenging new task that they could learn from!

The new test had problems that were harder to solve than the ones in the first test. The students didn't do so well this time. The students who were initially praised for their ability now didn't see themselves as so smart anymore. If success had meant they were intelligent, then less-than-success meant they were deficient.

However, the students who had been praised for their efforts simply thought that the difficulty meant they just had to work harder next time. They didn't see it as a failure, and they didn't think it reflected on their intellect.

Now here's the interesting part: after the experience with difficulty, the performance of the students who had initially been praised for their ability plummeted. Even when they were given easier problems to solve!

They lost faith in their ability and they did worse than when they started.

The effort students, on the other hand, showed better and better performance.

What is Your Mindset?

So what kind of mindset do you have? Fixed or growth?

If you take pride in your intelligence, skills or capabilities, and react to a setback defensively, making up excuses, you probably have a fixed mindset.

When you believe your abilities are carved in stone – because of the fixed mindset – you don't believe human qualities, such as behavioral change, can be cultivated through effort.

And that is not a good trait to have if you set challenging goals for yourself and seek to achieve them.

It's like you are trying to walk, to move forward, but you are constantly held back by a little kid pulling your shirt from the back. That kid doesn't want you to change.

As Dweck said in an interview with Harvard Business Review: *"In a growth mindset, challenges are exciting rather than threatening. So rather than thinking, oh, I'm going to reveal my weaknesses, you say, wow, here's a chance to grow"*.

This is the way you want to look at things when you are trying to set goals and achieve them.

Learning and trying to apply accelerated learning techniques while simultaneously cultivating a fixed mindset is like trying to row a boat that is still attached to the pier. You won't get very far...

Chapter 4: Let's Get Practical! Four Simple Techniques To Learn Faster

Okay, time to get our feet wet. Here are four easy and practical ways in which you can learn faster!

Mind Mapping

Mind mapping uses diagrams to visually organize data. This takes advantage of how your brain naturally processes information. If you observe your mind, for example in meditation, you'll observe that an image leads to a thought, which results in recalling a memory, which in turn triggers a certain emotion, et cetera: it's all connected, around a central axis, like spokes on a wheel.

Mind mapping helps to connect the dots between two or more things. Instead of randomly trying to memorize everything, it's much more effective to sort the information into groups and subgroups. This technique is effective for all learners, but if you are a visual learner (more about that later), this one is especially good for you!

Chunking

Our brain is wired to look for patterns. You can take advantage of that tendency to group information, to memorize it more easily. By breaking down information into little chunks, retention and recall become much easier. For example, it's much easier to remember a telephone number as 46 45 958 306 than 4-6-4-5-9-5-8-3-0-6.

Allegedly, Mozart even used this technique to write out *Miserere mei, Deus*, composed by Gregorio Allegri.

After hearing it only twice...The music was owned by the Vatican, who had forbidden its publication. However, luckily for Mozart, the work was really quite conventional and it is not difficult to chunk large portions of it around its standard features.

Link Items With Places and Images

If you can activate different parts of your brain to remember something, it will be much easier to memorize it. For example, a list of groceries only consists of words. But what if you could combine it with a place and imagery?

Let's say you have five items on the list:

- Cheese
- Lettuce
- Shampoo
- Toast
- Chocolate

Now, close your eyes for a second and associate each item with a room in your house:

- Living Room: place the cheese on the couch
- Kitchen: place the lettuce next to the sink
- Garden: place the shampoo on the grass
- Bathroom: place the lettuce under the shower
- Bedroom: place the chocolate in the socks drawer

Now imagine yourself walking through each room, observing the objects and where you've placed them.

Notice how I suggest you put the shampoo on the grass, and not in the bathroom. And how I suggest to put the chocolate in the socks drawer, and not in the kitchen. This is intentional: the weirder the place for the item on the grocery list, the more likely it is you are going to remember it. Try it for yourself!

Do the Opposite of What You are Doing That's Not Working

In his book *Hyperfocus*, Chris Bailey differentiates between two types of focus:

- **Hyperfocus**: the most productive mode of our brain. This is where you single mindedly focus on one thing, blocking out everything else
- **Scatterfocus**: the most creative mode of our brain. This is where you intentionally let your attention scatter to focus on nothing in particular.

When we're trying to be productive and *crush it*, hyperfocus often is the best mode to use. But sometimes you're just stuck and, no matter how hard you try, you can't come up with a solution.

The solution might be to do something counterintuitive. To do the opposite:

- Take a day off and go to the park
- Do something new and exciting
- Read a novel
- Play a musical instrument

At the surface level, it may seem that you've stopped working. But that's an illusion: your brain continues processing all that information you've worked on in hyperfocus mode. Now that you allow your brain to work in scatterfocus mode, it can start connecting all the dots and come up with answers you weren't able to find when you were hyperfocused.

Have you ever had a 'Eureka' moment when you were taking a shower, or in the gym? That's what can happen when you do the opposite of what's not working!

Chapter 5: How to Create A Positive Working And Learning Environment

Becoming better at learning isn't just a matter of learning a few tips and tricks.

Fear of failure is a disease. It eats away at personal achievement, self-confidence, and self-esteem. It affects decision making, leading to poor choices and an over-reliance on what is perceived as safe, but is in reality just making the call which leads to the least action. If we do nothing, then we can do nothing wrong. Of course, at the same time, we can do nothing right.

Fear of failure can impact everybody. You know the scenarios. In schools, students do not try to challenge themselves because they know they can get the teacher to give them the answers, and if the teacher does their work for them, then it will be right. The issue is that as a result, they will be unable to ever work independently. You know the saying – give a man a fish and you feed him for a day, but give him a fishing rod, and you feed him forever.

In work, you do not take on the extra staff member, because it might end up that there is not enough demand for their services. You do not take on the extra client in case you cannot cope with the work. You do not go for the promotion because you fear it will go to somebody else.

But this fear of failure can be addressed, and doing so is one of the key tenets required to achieve accelerated learning.

Create A Stimulating Environment

It is a well-known and accepted scientific fact that a stimulating environment enhances creativity. It encourages people to try new ideas, it gets the brain working in new and exciting ways.

In his book *Willpower Doesn't Work*, Benjamin Hardy even goes so far as to proclaim that **you are who you are because of your environment**.

"Because" is a highly successful media-branding organization with offices across the world. Enter their office and it is like moving into a theme park. Computer terminals sit among full size horses, a bus shelter, a train carriage. Color is all, bright and random (although, much less random than appears; as with all else, the design of the creative center is planned to the last detail). Treats are everywhere. There are bowls of sweets, bottles of beer, coffee machines, soft drinks; a comfortable relaxation area with soft, reclining seats turns out, in fact, to be a major meeting and training room.

Staff are dressed in a relaxed way. We know, scientifically, that in order for us to function at our best cognitively – in other words, to get our reasoning brain functioning at maximum velocity, our limbic brain needs to be satisfied. One of the factors to consider in achieving this is that of physical comfort. Casual clothing helps you to feel more comfortable than a tight tie or closely buttoned shirt and unyielding shoes. Consider how this view counters absolutely the traditional view of office dress.

In practical terms, there are many things that you can do to help create your stimulating working environment. While it does depend on where that environment might be and the control you have over it, the use of color can be very important. I once visited a school that catered to emotionally disturbed students. The calming impact hit as soon as the door opened. A gentle, soft sounding bell rang with a deep note to indicate a visitor had entered. Pastel grey walls led to a physical awareness of stress leaving the body. Wind chimes, fresh plants, doors "shushing" open – everything contributed to the sense of calm that had been created. Some environments need this effect. Others benefit from vibrant colors, strategically placed posters that appear random but in fact provide inspiration and information – such an environment will allow creativity to flourish. It is known that humans absorb information they see regularly – that notion of the power of imagery is one of the tenets of accelerated learning. Informational posters, changed or re-positioned regularly, will help to communicate the message you want to give.

It can seem unimportant, the environment in which you work. As long as there is a desk, a computer terminal, and so forth, so the opportunity is there to do your job. But applying the theory of accelerated learning to improving the functionality of that work will lead to better results. If you can, see if you can visit two schools, and the point is almost certainly going to become apparent. Firstly, ask if you can have a tour of a school catering to the youngest students, the six-year-olds and younger. You will be confronted by a blaze of excitement, color, work; a variety of resources. You will be stimulated. Then, by comparison, ask to visit a high school. Although many such schools have pockets of stimulating display, overall the effect will be much more neutral. Your own response will be less emotional. If you can recreate that elementary school environment, there will be an impact on the creativity of your workplace, and yourself.

Establish an Atmosphere Where Failure Is Fine

A fear of failure is one of the most destructive states that can exist in school, the office, or life in general. But this state can be countered. Many of us have been conditioned through our schooling, through our college education, and through our work to regard failure as a disaster. However, given enough support, we can emerge, like a frightened snail from its shell, to conquer the world in front of us.

If you think about it sensibly, if success always comes, then the challenge has been insufficient. Only through truly testing ourselves, through getting it wrong sometimes, can we really learn. Starting with this point of view, it is possible to begin to see the occasional failure as a good thing, provided learning from the experience occurs.

As manager, teacher, or leader, such values should be communicated regularly. This needs to be not only in words, but in actions. Posters outlining the importance of risking failure, encouragement to try again when ideas go wrong, and effective coaching to help others work out for themselves how to solve problems leads to students, workers – all of us in fact – becoming prepared to take risks, to learn from mistakes and become much more effective in our own progress in whatever field we are working or studying.

As the recipient of the benefits of valuing failure as well as success, you become more confident, more independent, and more lateral in your thinking.

It is true that accepting failure as the first step to success is alien to many, but the institution that encourages this approach will, ultimately, see improved learning (and therefore success) in their workforce.

Accepting failure as a part of the learning process takes time. However, reinforcing it with physical reminders and backing this up with your own approach to failure – your own or that of others – will soon see you regarding failure as something more than negative; as the first step towards accelerating your own learning.

The Secret to Achieving Your Goals: Enjoyment

It's a strange but very common state of mind that work is not something to enjoy. But you spend so much of your life at work, or school, or college, that it is madness that such time should not be spent happily, for the most part, at least.

There is physical enjoyment. Having good coffee, providing comfortable furnishings, holding a dress code that liberates rather than inhibits. But more powerful is the emotional enjoyment that can enhance your creativity.

Good relationships with others, developing a sense of your own progress, and the self-esteem that this brings – these are the characteristics needed if you are to accelerate your own learning with a sense of your enjoyment.

Perhaps the single biggest impact on your enjoyment of your work is your own PMA – positive mental attitude. Somebody who regards their study, their employment, or whatever it might be with positivity will be more stimulated, more engaged, and happier than somebody who sees it as just a job, or as just school or college.

So, how to develop this PMA?

Firstly, concentrating on the present is important. Yes, our present is shaped by our past and guided by our future goals, but we live in the now, so that is what is most important. It is human nature to worry that things will go wrong. Usually they do not. And when they do, it is very rare that we do not cope with them. So, live in the now, not the then or the time to come. It will help.

Secondly, the language that you use can help to shape your mental attitude. Is it often negative? Do you often express the faults of others, the failures of systems, the hard work you do for little reward? Or do you use language that is positive? The thing is, somebody who is negative draws the energy out of other people. As a result, those vital emotional connections we establish with friends, loved ones, family, associates, and so forth are less strong. But conversely, somebody who is upbeat, who sees opportunities not problems, invigorates those around them. There is a theory called The Law of Attraction that states that we naturally veer towards people who mirror our attitudes. That means that somebody who is negative attracts other negative people to them. The result is a sense of misery, of pointlessness in what they do. But somebody who is positive engages with other positive people, and that is the recipe for creativity and progress.

Another key to maximizing our PMA is to accept that not everything will be perfect. A part of this is the willingness to embrace failure, but the concept goes further. At the end of the day, you cannot control everything – none of us can – and nor should we want to. What will be will be, and by accepting that, negative thoughts are kept at bay. Yes, there are times when things are bad, but mostly they pass in the end.

Curiosity helps to develop a positive mental attitude, and that curiosity involves a willingness to learn all the time. Being a writer is an incredibly fulfilling job; it is deeply satisfying. A part of that is because writers are learning all the time. They are discovering new information and improving their ways of communicating that learning. Ask most teachers what they enjoy most about their jobs and they will tell you it is working with young people, because they are so positive to be around. Of course, young people are learning all the time – their curiosity is constantly stimulated and satisfied, and that makes them positive.

Finally, developing a positive mental attitude involves being grateful. Be grateful for your strengths and show that gratitude by helping others – even the little things can make you feel positive. Some people take this notion of gratitude further and keep a gratitude journal. It is a good idea if you are a person seeking to improve your own positivity. Keep it daily, writing down the things that made you smile, that made you realize that life is not so bad. When your positivity is wearing thin, you can return to the journal and re-read past entries, seeing that in context, things are actually pretty good.

A Positive Environment Is A Safe Environment

If a person is worried, scared, or anxious, their learning is going to be impacted. That is common sense. A vital tenet of accelerated learning is that the environment in which learning takes place should be safe.

Now, you would be a very strange person – and certainly not interested in improving yourself or others – if you consciously sought to create an environment that is unsafe. However, such an outcome can result inadvertently. Frequently, it is not something that is realized.

If you are responsible for your learning environment, then you can make a difference. But even if you are not, your own attitude can have a positive influence on others. The biggest inadvertent factor leading to an unsafe environment is competition. It brings out the worst in people. For every winner, there will be many losers, and none of us wishes to be that. Being a loser impacts our self-esteem, makes us feel bad about ourselves, and makes us seek ways to become a winner using any method possible. It is not only harmful to ourselves, but also to the institution in which we operate.

For accelerated learning to take place, the environment for learning must be non-competitive. Indeed, it must be collaborative. Mutual support breeds good relationships and makes us feel good about ourselves.

Imagine we are seeking to learn ways to improve our sales figures in a company. The bosses have set targets, with rewards for the best sales figures. They think that they are providing motivation to their workforce because they themselves have been competitive throughout their lives. Let's assume that they have a team of twenty sales people.

During the first month, perhaps half of that team might feel that they have a chance of winning and seek ways to maximize their sales. But, they are under pressure; they can't get it wrong or they fail. And failure means defeat. The other half of the team just ticks away in an unmotivated manner, achieving very little because they know that they can never win, but since the others are engaged by the challenge, overall sales figures are good.

By month two, the previous month's winner is under pressure to maintain their success. A couple of opponents feel that they have a chance. But for the remaining seventeen, victory is impossible, and they are demotivated by the target. Overall, sales figures are lower. The pattern is clear.

Now consider if those bosses did not create a competition but rather set a team goal. Everybody is now playing a part in the success. Good practice is shared, not kept as a secret; clients are not closely guarded and perhaps lost because a person cannot give them the time needed. Instead, clients are shared, with those who have time to give them taking on their business. Overall, those twenty sales people sell much more than they would as twenty separate units; they feel good about their work and possess the motivation that comes from being a part of closely-knit team.

If somebody tries something new and it does not work, then that is fine because other members of the team will cover for them. If their new concept is a success, it is readily shared with the remainder of the team, to the benefit of all.

It does not matter whether we are talking about a sales office, a classroom, a college assignment or a business, collaboration is simply more successful than competition. It is so blindingly obvious that it is astonishing that the idea is not more widely accepted. That is why collaboration is a central part of accelerated learning.

While it is one of the most common ways of making an environment unsafe, collaboration is not the only thing that contributes to the necessary safe conditions for accelerated learning (or, for that matter, any kind of learning) to be effective.

A workplace needs to be free from bullying and harassment. Clearly, a competitive environment promotes these negative and dangerous attributes. A competitive environment encourages there to be a top dog and a series of victims.

If you are in a position to influence or control the environment in which you operate, and you wish to ensure both accelerated learning and basic humanity, then it is necessary to ensure that such an environment is mentally and emotionally secure; also that it is physically and sexually secure – the allegations surrounding Harvey Weinstein and others in the entertainment industry demonstrate how easily such basic expectations can be breached. Bullying and harassment have no place in society, and proponents need to be challenged and their behavior addressed.

To be honest, if you are trying to learn in an environment in which you do not feel safe and the attitudes and values that promote that lack of safety are so ingrained that they cannot be changed, then the best thing is to leave that environment. Fortunately, our schools and colleges are often sufficiently accountable these days to ensure that complaints be properly addressed, but that is not always the case, and especially not in the workplace. Sometimes, moving on is all that can be done. The results will be better for you in the end.

In this chapter, the important role of a safe and stimulating environment as a part of accelerated learning has been studied. You have learned what constitutes such a learning environment and how it can go wrong. You have had some practical guidance on how to create a stimulating environment, and how to ensure it is as safe as possible.

Next, we'll consider the importance of total learner involvement as a key part of ensuring accelerated learning.

Chapter 6: The Trick to Learning Like a Pro

There is an old Chinese saying and it translates something like this:

> *"I hear...and I forget.*
> *I see...and I remember.*
> *I do...and I understand."*

Accelerated learning challenges the traditional notion of learning. That is, that an expert imparts their knowledge to a group of willing acolytes who hang on every word and absorb that knowledge.

Traditional Learning is Boring

Anybody who remembers their school days, their college days, or that interminable in-service training session they were forced to attend will know the truth. Fundamentally, listening is boring. For it not to be, firstly, the speaker needs to be of stunningly good quality, offering engaging content in manageable chunks. Sadly, few people are this good at speaking. Next, human brains take time to digest and analyze information. They need to sort content into ways that they can retain, and that usually involves questions, literal or rhetorical. The brain cannot do all of this while being continuously bombarded with new data.

We can also apply some science to see the shortfall of the lecture as a means of imparting learning. Scientists are still learning about the brain, but what they do know is that for information to be properly placed into long-term or even working memory, there needs to be an *emotional* response from the recipient to the information they are receiving. Certainly, the sense of hearing is being used to access the data, but the bottom line is if you or I are bored by what we are being subjected to, if we are not engaged by it, we will not remember it.

You probably will have sat through long, hot, and uncomfortable sessions where your attention quickly moved from what is being said to other matters – watching other people, playing a game on your phone, or simply dreaming away until the session thankfully, mercifully ends.

Visual Aids Help, But…

Although learning fails to be imparted through lectures far too often than is good for the recipient, at least educationalists have learned that visual aids can assist learning. The old Chinese saying at the beginning of the chapter might be a little kind to the "seeing" aspect, since we probably forget more than we remember, but we do still at least recall information better when we have seen it as opposed to only hearing it.

Where lecturing, even with visual aids, fails is that the learner is not actively engaged by the process of learning. He or she is passive in the process, whereas accelerated learning only occurs when the learner is active in the acquisition of knowledge, experiences, or skills. Again, this is true whether we are talking about young children or adults learning new techniques for their work. Certainly, young children generally have shorter concentration spans than adults, but even in adults, research suggests that after twenty minutes, a change of focus is needed.

The Trick: Get Active!

So, we can see that accelerated learning involves getting active as quickly as possible. Studying a play from Shakespeare? Act it. Learning about quadratic equations? Work on examples. Acquiring new plumbing skills? Get practical with your monkey wrench and bath taps. Developing ways to market your brand? Find a piece of paper or some suitable software and get designing.

In fact, this last point is an important one for the whole concept of accelerated learning. Not only does the brain absorb images quickly and well, but the process of creating pictures helps understanding and absorption of information. Drawing, and to a lesser extent, writing about the subject is a good tool to aid learning.

However, the point here is that if we wish to achieve accelerated learning, we need to DO and not just RECEIVE. You must be ACTIVE and not PASSIVE. It is important to be INVOLVED and not REMOTE.

Of course, like all the best things in life, the different elements of accelerated learning are interlinked and self-supporting. When we DO rather than RECEIVE, we are far more likely to be collaborative, and that is a key to this kind of learning. We are more likely to enjoy ourselves and feel positive, which are also vital attributes. And as we develop our response to getting it wrong, failure becomes less of a problem and more of an opportunity, because we have time to repair and improve upon our mistakes.

There is a good deal of science behind this theory, as well. It is now known that learning takes place on many levels at once. If we are simply listening to a lecture, even if we are able to maintain some semblance of focus, then the only sense we are using to learn is our hearing. But if we are doing, being active, then we use many senses simultaneously. We use our sight through seeing what we are doing and what needs to be done, we use our hearing in listening to feedback and hearing the results of what we are doing, we use touch, perhaps we even use smell and taste. We learn consciously through reading instructions and discussing our work. We also learn subconsciously as we see what works and what does not. We constantly assess and evaluate our progress.

So, the lessons are clear. If you are looking to improve the skills of others through accelerated learning because you are acting as an educator or trainer, then ensure that the training and teaching you give involves students and recipients getting their hands dirty. Ensure that they are active and not passive in their learning. We don't learn how to swim from a book. We learn it by getting in the pool.

Feedback

There is an additional factor to aid accelerated learning when you become an active learner, and that is the important element of feedback. Teachers and trainers are not made redundant by accelerated learning; in fact, they become even more important. Since you have created something as a part of your learning, getting feedback on it from the expert is extremely valuable. It makes that feedback personal to you, allowing you to work specifically on what you need to do to improve further.

If you are controlling your own learning, seek ways where you can be practical. Do rather than just read, involve yourself rather than just watch. Talk to others rather than work as an island.

In this chapter, you have studied the importance of active learning to accelerate your acquisition of skills and knowledge. So, to avoid the irony of just reading about the importance of being active in your learning, do something! Summarize the main points. Use color to create a mind map of what you have studied – a mind map is like a spider chart where all the points are listed in key words or phrases and connections are made between them with lines. Those lines can be color-coded to pick up themes. If you enjoy being creative, deliver the lessons you have learned so far to an audience or make a recording or video of them.

Draw a picture of your key findings. Share the chapter, or even the book, with a friend and discuss your thoughts.

In the next chapter, we will explore the ways in which people learn, as well as how offering a variety of learning techniques is another key factor in the acquisition of accelerated learning.

Chapter 7: Different Learning Styles And How You Can Use Them

There are many ways to learn. Some systems work better for some than for others, but there are benefits to be gained from all techniques. Even listening to a lecture offers some benefit.

Do you remember completing endless English grammar exercises as a child? Occasionally, they were probably quite fun. They involved actively doing something and they were not too difficult, so it was easy to succeed; they were repetitive and familiar. To do them every lesson, had your teacher been so disposed, would be frustrating, boring, and educationally suspect. But as an occasional lesson, it worked. At the end of these lessons, you could probably recognize superlatives and comparatives; your use of the apostrophe was almost certainly improved.

In this chapter, you will learn more about the various learning styles that exist and see how the application of a variety of these is crucial in the delivery and acquisition of accelerated learning.

Visual Learners

Visual learners, sometimes called spatial learners, favor using color, pictures, images, and maps to support their learning. Often, people who like to learn visually can identify themselves because they hold a very strong sense of direction.

One trick when learning visually is to create mind maps. Here, the information you need to learn can be held by the map, and the use of colors or small pictures on the map will help information to stick in your head.

A second way to learn is to create cartoons or story maps of the information you need to hold, as these will remain more firmly in your head than textual information.

Visual learning is especially effective for engineering or mechanical projects. If you are not a natural visual learner, developing the technique through experience and practice will help with these practical types of activities.

Aural Learners

Aural learners feel the beat. They identify the natural rhythm of language, and this helps them to store and recall information. They are good learners of lists and sets of facts, being able to develop mnemonics, acrostics, and rhythmic lines to store information.

Sounds recall information for this type of learner and will offer triggers that set thoughts in motion. Aural learners make use of their musical abilities to create catchy jingles and apply information in the form of tunes to make them more memorable.

For those who are not natural aural learners, practice will make them better at preparing for exams and tests, and for learning information that is factual or in list form.

Physical Learners

This type of learning is sometimes called kinesthetic learning. Physical learners like to be active. Taking into account what was covered earlier, physical learners access accelerated learning easily, because of their love of active participation. Physical learners would, in the olden days, and still (in the worst schools) in the present, be the sort of children who failed at traditional schooling.

Sitting down and listening would be torture to them, something to which they struggled to adapt. They would be the learners identified as troublesome or lacking in focus. They wanted – needed – to be out running around, making models and working physically rather than listening to abstract ideas.

An example is Gillian Lynne. Among other things, she was a ballerina, and created the theatre choreography for the very successful Broadway shows Cats and The Phantom of the Opera. However, if it wasn't for the advice of her doctor when she was 13 years old, her life could have unfolded very differently. Her mother had taken her to the doctor because she had been underperforming at school. After hearing her mother out, the doctor told Lynne he needed to talk to her mother in private. Before they walked out, he turned on the radio. Once they were in the other room, the doctor said to her mother: *"Look at Lynne, she is dancing to the music on the radio. She is a dancer, take her to a dance school."* And the rest is history...

Physical learners should concentrate on what things feel like. If they are learning a new skill, they should focus on what performing an action actually does to them. Sometimes, they struggle with writing and drawing, but can work on these, as they are still physical activities and as such can become things to love.

Naturally physical learners are good at making things, good at gardening and at traditional trades because they can sense what is right and what is not. Those who do not readily learn in this way should practice because doing so will enhance their practical skills, providing the sort of daily life skills that are useful (fixing a tap, building a bookshelf, repairing a lawn mower) and also will add a different form of learning to their overall capacity, making them more effective accelerated learners in the long run.

Verbal Learners

Sometimes called linguistic learners, verbal learners are those who traditionally do well in school. They are the people who love to read and enjoy writing. They can absorb and process textual information.

Often less good at the practical side of life (something they should address if they want to become accelerated learners), they nevertheless achieve well because they can take in information in any textual form and are good at debating and rationalizing their ideas.

Those who are not good at this kind of learning style can find it hard to acquire. They should seek to read material that is of interest to them – short articles and fact books are often better than complex literature. They should be happy with writing concisely, understanding that it is quality rather than quantity that wins the day.

Without good verbal learning skills, the world of books, discussions, and instructions are to an extent lost, and although it may not be right that these skills are valued highly in schools, most workplaces, and in life as a whole, everybody does have to live within those constraints, and make the best of it. Positive mental attitude – "I need to read so I am going to do it. And I'm going to enjoy the process."

Logical Learners

If any learning style is to challenge the verbal form as the most highly regarded, it is logical learning, sometimes called mathematical learning.

Logical learners do very well on tests and exams. They can easily spot patterns and solve problems. Numbers are a joy, rather than a detriment, to them. Logical learners are often good aural learners, as well.

The main danger with this kind of style is that there can be a tendency to learn by rote, without acquiring full understanding, because it is something these kinds of people find easy. That will come back to bite them as the concepts become more challenging.

Logical learners are good at science, good at math, and strong at puzzles. Those who are not as inclined to this type of learning can improve by playing strategy games which help to develop logic. There are many such electronic and online games, and even old patience card games will help to develop logical skills. So, will trying the sorts of number puzzles that are popular today, such as code words (which are numerical even though they involve letters) and sudoku. Learning to play strategy games such as Risk, chess, or checkers will also help in a fun way, as well as give you the choice of learning the rules in your preferred style.

Social Or Solitary Learning

The final two main learning styles are best considered together. Once again, to achieve the best results from accelerated learning, it is wise to become comfortable with both, even though they are direct opposites, because at times, each of the styles will become the most appropriate to employ.

Social learners enjoy debate. They enjoy talking through concepts with their peers. They enjoy working collaboratively and solving problems or meeting targets. As we saw earlier, this is a key tenet for success in accelerated learning. Solitary learning does, though, retain a small place. Sometimes that information studied has to be stored firmly in the mind. Quiet, personal study will help to reinforce something that has been understood through working collaboratively. Certainly, social learning is more important, but just like the final dash of turmeric in your curry, there might not be too much of it, but you notice if it is not there.

Each of the other five types of learning can be social or solitary. Those who are naturally social learners tend to become better at jobs involving people, communication, or care. By contrast, solitary learners will like work that they can get on with by themselves, such as accountancy tasks.

In this chapter, you have seen that there are seven learning styles. You have come to learn that everybody is naturally inclined towards some styles more than others, but there is value in becoming efficient at all of these methods of acquiring information and skills. Then, the best style can be adapted for the specific task at hand.

Accelerated learners are comfortable with all learning styles and have experience with all of them, which they use to maximize their ability to deal with the new and the challenging.

Next up, you will learn about the importance of learning in context.

Chapter 8: Accelerated Learning and the Importance of Context

Sadly, it is the traditional style in schools, in colleges, and in workplace training (admittedly to a lesser extent) to be presented with new learning in abstract ways. Workplace training does have, at least, the context of relating to your work, but even so, the teaching is often presented out of the context of the place in which you operate.

Remember that historically, education has been about the expert imparting knowledge which the recipient should acquire, rather than the idea that the learner takes charge of their own learning. However, we have known since the 1980s, from the work of (among others) Jean Lave and Etienne Wenger, that this is not the best way for people to develop understanding.

Symbol Process Learning

Traditional learning styles are sometimes known as "symbol process" learning. In other words, everything is transmitted via a kind of code; be it verbal, written, or mathematical. What is happening is that the teacher is informing their students through abstract ideas about the things they have decided those students should know. We can illustrate this point with two examples, one for classroom learning, one for professional learning.

Let's take the idea that a class of high school students is learning about the Amazon basin. The teacher gives them the information through books, perhaps even slides or a video. But the students are sitting in a classroom. The details their brains are trying to process do not in any way relate to the experiences they are having. How can a teacher put these ideas in context? One idea is to employ a field trip; practically, it might not be possible to visit the Amazon basin, but the principles are the same with other large rivers, which are perhaps more accessible.

The same idea can be illustrated as a work place scenario, as identified by the University of Northern Illinois in contemporary research they carried out. The example the university uses is of a person training to work in child care. Teaching about child care in a classroom is removed from the reality of what it is like. The noises, smells, and pressures are all completely different in a classroom than when working in a child care setting. However, if "working centers" are set up, then students can learn in real situations, with practical experiences that are meaningful and memorable. We see this in teaching hospitals, where young doctors get first-hand experience working with patients at a level suitable for their growing skills and knowledge.

The same can also apply to workplace experience. After all, learning the skills of an electrician is better done "on the job" than simply learning theory in the classroom.

Symbol Process Learning – Not For Everyone

Research suggests that a small percentage of the population, maybe around a third, do work well with symbol process learning; these tend to be the students who learn effectively using linguistic or logical approaches. Physical learners, along with well over half a typical population, do not work well with this type of learning. For these people, failure is reinforced by symbol process learning, but this is not failure that leads to new and improved learning, such as is advocated under accelerated learning principles. No, it is failure that is negative, failure in a competitive environment which wrecks self-esteem and demotivates its victims.

However, what is interesting is that although certain groups of students do succeed with symbol processing learning, they succeed even more when that learning is put in context.

Accelerated Learning in Context

What is most probably behind the tendency towards a reluctance to situate learning in schools and colleges, even workplace training, is cost. However, those supporters of accelerated learning, who believe that learning needs to be put in context – situated, in other words – would argue that not putting learning in context is like buying the cheapest ingredients and wine for an important dinner. Sure, the guests get fed, but the meal's mediocre at best and many will not like it at all. However, if you buy the best ingredients, everybody gets a great meal. Surely, the education of our young people makes a little extra spending (and re-prioritization of what is actually learned) worthwhile?

In a practical sense, we have discovered that accelerated learning occurs when learning is in context. The point fits with the idea of doing rather than receiving, being active rather than passive in your studies. This means that, for example, if you want to teach your kids about the Civil War, you should take them to a battlefield reenactment or a museum rather than give them a book to read.

If you wish to develop your own handyman skills, get to work on something real (that can be remedied if you go wrong). Put up those shelves, rather than just read about how to do it. If you do go wrong, then you will learn from your mistakes. If you get it right, the actions you followed will stick more fully in your memory.

In the workplace, the argument is even stronger. Proper training in a situated context will deliver skills and knowledge to workers in a way that will ensure economic returns to businesses, and the economy as a whole, making money in the long run.

Chapter 9: Metacognition – The Key To Effective Accelerated Learning

Have you ever bought a book on a subject, or found a website or online course, and been disappointed that the results did not meet the expectations you set? It would be unusual not to have experienced this. The thing is, you know what you want to know – it is just that *finding the answer* can be a challenge. But for students, whether in schools, colleges, or workplace training, somebody else is deciding what they need to know.

And have you ever tried to teach somebody something? Maybe you've helped your sibling, child, or the neighbor's kid with their math homework. You know what they need to know, but they don't get it. Yet, it is simple. You can't see where they are going wrong, and they can't pick up the points you are trying to get across.

It's so frustrating—for both of you. Indeed, such is that frustration that soon voices begin to rise. You use that dogmatic tone that says, *"Do as I say, because I am the expert."* They use that *"You don't get it because you're an idiot"* tone in which youngsters specialize. Or worse, they go quiet and moody prior to slamming the books closed and storming to their room.

The reason for the frustration is that your student, or your colleague, or whoever, does not really know where they are going wrong, and cannot verbalize their problem. If they could, you might be able to advise, or better still, give them practical guidance. But they cannot communicate their difficulties, while you perfectly understand the concept you are trying to teach and have no idea why your poor subject cannot get it, as well.

Metacognitive Learning

The answer is to develop metacognitive learning in young people. This skill, which is the highest form of learning, and is accelerated learning by any other name, is, once acquired, something that stays for life.

Meta means "with" or "beyond" and cognitive means "understanding." So, people who learn metacognitively do so with understanding.

The process to becoming a metacognitive learner fits very closely with those methods that help people's learning to become accelerated. Indeed, many of the facets of accelerated learning, such as self-esteem, positive mental attitude, and so forth, deliver the emotional needs required to become metacognitive.

The first step is to be as independent in your learning as you can. So, using our earlier example, get your child to do their math homework. Encourage them to try to complete the subtraction exercises. Reassure them that it does not matter if they get a few wrong – indeed, it will help them. This is not easy, because they are trained from a very young age to see failure as something negative, especially in school. That training needs to be overcome, and this can take time. You can start by encouraging them to take on the exercise, because by doing so, they are being active in their learning, not passively listening to instruction.

Encourage them to try different methods. For example, there are many ways to solve subtraction problems. Consider the problem 174 minus 89. Here, you can use the traditional column method, which is probably the way most people would find the answer. You can chunk, or in other words, add blocks of number until the answer is reached. You could count up from the lower number to the higher. You could use a table method, where several calculations are made. For example, four minus nine equals negative five. 70 minus 80 is negative 10. 100 minus nothing is 100. 100 minus 10 is 90. 90 minus five is 85. Which is, of course, the answer to the sum.

Each of those methods works. So, one system is no better than the other, even if it is not the way you would do it. If it works for your kid, then understanding is gained.

Eventually, over time, learners become properly independent. They are not afraid of getting it wrong because they know that they will use this to help them get it right. Then, magic occurs. They begin to know what they do not know. Once they can identify this, they can ask the questions to fill their knowledge gaps or find the answer through their own research.

Ultimately, this leads them to become properly metacognitive in their learning. They know what they need to know, they know what it is they need to do to acquire such knowledge or skills, and they have the means to access those missing pieces of their intellectual jigsaw puzzle, whether that means asking questions, getting on the web, finding a book, discussing with their peers, or even getting practical.

Properly metacognitive learners are the most successful students, they are the workers who make the most progress in their careers, and everything else being equal, they are the people who acquire the best and widest life skills.

And the method they use to make such progress? It is, of course, accelerated learning.

In this chapter, you have learned about the highest form of learning, metacognitive learning, and how this system reflects the various tenets of accelerated learning.

In the final chapter, you will see some more tips and techniques to help you acquire your own skills in becoming an accelerated learner.

Chapter 10: More Practical Tips for Accelerating Your Own Learning

Here are have some tips to try to live by on your own journey towards becoming an accelerated learner. If you are sharing your knowledge with others, then always remember the key elements outlined in earlier chapters.

Teaching Others Teaches Yourself

By teaching a skill or some knowledge you are acquiring to another person, you actually teach yourself. The process of communicating that information helps you to clarify your own thinking; it helps to prioritize the important information and it helps you to solve problems you have in your own head.

Question

Asking questions helps you identify what you are still trying to clarify. Very often, the act of asking the question will give you the answer you seek. You probably know the feeling. You email a request to a colleague, and then immediately send a *"Don't worry, I've got it"* follow up. Simply recognizing and posing the question will often lead you to the answer you seek.

Have A Conversation…With Yourself

We noted earlier that holding a conversation with others is a key part of accelerated learning, but we have also noted that some people are solitary learners, and also that at times we need to be by ourselves to get a concept firmly entrenched in our minds. Even if you are a solitary learner or you don't have access to someone else, you can still have that conversation. Talking clarifies thoughts; your mind holds huge amounts of detail in its subconscious and talking brings that information into your conscious mind. So, talk to yourself, describing the learning you are seeking to achieve. Just make sure you close the door first.

Get Out the Colored Crayons

Remember that accelerated learning requires you to use all learning styles. Some people will naturally create pictures to help them remember and understand. Others will not. Especially if they regard themselves as bad at art. But not only will putting something in image form help it to be remembered, but the act of drawing engages different elements of the brain from reading or reasoning. And the more of our brains we use, the more successful we will be.

Keep Motivated

Positive mental attitude is, as you know, key. But sometimes it is difficult to be positive. Let's say you are preparing for a big presentation at work; let's be honest, you know you need to do it, but it is very boring. You'd rather be at the gym or watching a film.

Keep your end goal present and visual. Write it down. Pin it on your wall. Stick it to your desk. Make it your computer screensaver. Maybe giving a good presentation will lead to a rise in salary and you will be able to afford that car you have wanted since it hit the market. Print off a picture of it and put it in your line of sight to remind you why you are working.

Another thing about PMA: it makes you feel good. Chemically, being positive releases pleasure endorphins, which make you feel happy. It is a positive circle. Feel good and you release endorphins that make you feel even better, even more motivated. Conversely, remember, negative feelings release negative emotions. If it is very hard to get positive, exercise can really help. Go on a 30-minute walk and you will genuinely feel better.

If You Can't Do, Think

Putting learning in context and being practical are key elements of accelerated learning. But, even with the best will in the world, we cannot always be doing them. However, there is a trick that replicates the experiences almost as well. Let's say you are learning home skills. While sitting in traffic trying to get home from the office, it is not practical to be putting up bookshelves; they tend to be out of place in a car. However, you can visualize the process in your mind. You can think through the stages, solve the problems, and so forth mentally. It is not as good as doing, but it will help.

Remember, though, to think through all the senses. Remember how putting the screw in feels; how sawing the wood smells. Such sensory actions will really help to store the processes in your mind.

Move

Being active helps learning. Sometimes, simply doing the task will help you to remain active. But sometimes you will be sedentary. Make yourself move around. If working on the laptop, make sure that you go for a walk round the room or make a drink, have a snack or dust a shelf at least every half an hour. Physical activity keeps the brain working well.

Try to experiment with all these practical accelerated learning tools, depending on the task in hand. Becoming an accelerated learner requires challenging traditional ways of acquiring skills and knowledge, but it really works!

Final Words

You learned best as a child, because you learned by doing and weren't afraid to fail. Instead, you intuitively realized that learning is *only* possible through experiencing what *doesn't* work.

So, you had a growth mindset without realizing it. Yet, what was missing at the time were tools and techniques for smart, *accelerated* learning.

Now you have the best of both world: a framework to learn effectively, and the right mindset to accompany it, to deal with the roadblocks you'll inevitably encounter.

I hope you have enjoyed this book. If you want to continue learning about accelerated learning, I recommend you check out the Resources below.

If you apply what you've read, success in learning is pretty much guaranteed. Good luck!

Resources

- *Accelerated Learning for the 21st Century* – Colin Rose
- *Willpower Doesn't Work: Discover the Hidden Keys to Success* – Benjamin Hardy
- *Quantum Learning* – Bobbi DePorter
- *Peak Learning* – Ronald Gross
- *Super Teaching* – Eric Jensen
- *The Accelerated Learning Handbook* – Dave Meier
- *The Art of Learning: An Inner Journey to Optimal Performance* – Joshua Waitzkin
- *The Learning Revolution* – Gordon Dryden & Jeannette Vos
- *Accelerated Learning: How You Learn Determines What You Learn* – Roger Swartz

- *Hyper Focus: How To Be More Productive in a World of Distraction* – Chris Bailey

BONUS CHAPTER: What is Stoicism

Below, you will find a free bonus chapter from my book **'STOICISM FOR BEGINNERS**: *Master the Art of Happiness. Learn Modern, Practical Stoicism to Create Your Own Daily Stoic Routine.'*

Enjoy!

It is my way of saying thanks for

- *Reading this book, and*
- *Taking your first step on the path of Accelerated Learning. You rock!*

Let's get started, shall we?

***

In this chapter, you are going to learn what Stoicism is and where it originates.

In recent years, interest in the ancient philosophy of Stoicism has experienced a renaissance. Despite the growing popularity of this older philosophy, there are still so many misconceptions about it. For instance, many people believe that Stoicism is about being devoid of any emotion, including happiness. Others think that to be a stoic, you need to lead a Spartan and bland lifestyle. To set the records straight, let's take a look at what Stoicism really is.

What is Stoicism?

Stoicism is a philosophy that helps us maintain control over our thoughts and actions in a world full of chaos and unpredictability. Stoicism understands that we have no control over external occurrences, and therefore we should not rely on them. Instead, we should rely on our mind, behavior, and reaction to external events, all of which we can control. Stoicism teaches us that what matters is not what *happens* to us, but rather, how we *react* to it. In a world of chaos, Stoicism teaches us how to remain steadfast, strong and in control of ourselves.

Most of our dissatisfaction in life occurs because, rather than using logic, we have an impulsive dependency on our reflexes. Stoicism helps us to:

- overcome these destructive emotions,
- act on what we can act upon, and
- accept things that we cannot act upon.

Rather than being a philosophy of endless debate, Stoicism is **focused on action**.

The core principle of this ancient philosophy is that we need to overcome our insatiability in order for us to lead good and meaningful lives. Most people today live their lives like slaves, always in pursuit of happiness. Every person has a long list of desires that they are trying to satisfy. Even those you consider to have attained success have more things they want to achieve. The problem is that, once one desire is satisfied, it tends to be immediately replaced by a new one. This keeps most of us in continuous chase, always trying to satisfy our desires. After a lifetime of pursuit, we are no more satisfied than we were at the very start. This way, we end up wasting our lives instead of living for each moment.

Stoicism is a philosophy that should be applied in our day to day lives. It focuses on ethics (how we live our lives), which are in turn influenced by the natural world and logic. The resurgence of the popularity of Stoicism in the modern world has been driven by the fact that the philosophy aims to teach us how to attain peace, joy and tranquility in the midst of struggles and hardship.

The Origin of Stoicism

Stoicism was founded in Athens in the early 3rd century BC. The philosophy was founded by a Phoenician merchant and philosopher known as Zeno. Zeno was born in Citium, a town in Cyprus, and lived from 334 to 262 BC. At around the age of 34, during one of his travels, Zeno was shipwrecked. Luckily, he survived and found himself in Athens. Having lost everything and with nothing else to do in life, he visited a bookseller in Athens. It is here that he found a book that would lead him on the path of becoming a philosopher. After learning under Crates of Thebes and the philosophers of the Megarian School, he then began teaching and practicing his own philosophy. His school of philosophy was known as Zenoism, before the name was later changed to Stoicism. The name Stoicism was derived from the Stoa Poikile, a 'painted porch' from where Zeno used to give his lectures. His students became known as 'Stoics'.

Stoicism was not a philosophy that was reserved for the aristocrats. It was a philosophy of the street, open for ordinary people. A *working class* philosophy, if you will! Anyone could go to the Stoa Poikile and listen to the teachings of Zeno.

The philosophy taught and practiced by Zeno as well as other Stoic philosophers was heavily influenced by the works of Socrates. Apart from Socrates, Stoicism was also influenced by the Cynics, the Skeptics and the Academics (the followers of Plato).

While Stoicism was founded by Zeno, one of the most influential Greek Stoics was Chrysippus, who was one of Zeno's followers. Chrysippus is said to have elaborated most of the doctrines that are associated with the philosophy to this day. Apart from Plato, Socrates and Aristotle, Chrysippus is believed to be the greatest ancient philosopher. Though he is believed to have authored over 700 works, unfortunately none of them survived.

Despite having originated in ancient Greece, the greatest influence of Stoicism would be felt centuries later when it got to the Roman Empire. Most of what is known about Stoicism today comes from the ideas and writings of the Roman Stoics. Some of the most influential Stoics from this era include Epictetus, Musonius Rufus, Seneca and Marcus Aurelius.

Owing to the kind of lives led by the early Stoic philosophers, Stoicism was perceived as a very practical and very useful school of thought from its early stages. It later moved from Athens to the West, where it gained lots of popularity. However, the adoption of Christianity as the official Roman religion and its subsequent spread to the west led to the decline of Stoicism and several other ancient Greek philosophies. People abandoned this ancient philosophy to the point where it almost became extinct.

Fortunately, Stoic Philosophy started making a comeback in the late 20th Century. This resurgence has been driven by a number of factors. These include the adoption of the philosophy by celebrities and pop culture idols, featuring of the philosophy in the works of renowned authors as well as the growing interest in self-development. Some popular business and political leaders who have been known to practice Stoicism include Bill Gates, Warren Buffet, Tim Ferris, Tony Robbins, Presidents George Washington and Theodore Roosevelt, as well as actor/musician LL Cool J.

In the next chapter, you are going to learn the key beliefs and principles beliefs of Stoicism.

The Most Important Stoic Philosophers

In the next chapter, you are going to learn the beliefs and principles that form the foundation of the philosophy of Stoicism.

They are based on the teachings of three Stoic leaders:

- **Marcus Aurelius**: Aurelius was an Emperor of the Roman Empire, and the last one among the five so-called good Emperors. Perhaps you remember him from the first scenes of the 2000 movie *Gladiator*. During this time, Aurelius was the most powerful person on earth. He had everything under his command, he could fulfill any of his desires, yet he exercised great restraint against his temptations. Each evening, Marcus Aurelius sat down alone, reflected on his day and wrote his thoughts in a private diary. His diary was later published as the book *Meditations*. This book has been one of the most significant sources of knowledge about Stoic philosophy.

- **Epictetus**: Despite the fame he had attained by the time of his death, Epictetus was born as a slave. Epictetus discovered Stoicism through another Stoic philosopher known as Musonius

Rufus. When he gained his freedom, Epictetus founded his own school and went ahead to teach many great people in Rome, one of whom was Marcus Aurelius. Epictetus never wrote down his teachings. His influence came by pure luck through one of his students – Arrian – who wrote down his teachings. Arrian wrote two books, Discourses and Enchiridion, which contain most of the teachings of Epictetus.

- **Seneca**: Seneca was a renowned playwright, an advisor to emperor Nero, and one of the wealthiest people within the Roman Empire. Seneca was exposed to Stoicism by Attalus, a Stoic philosopher who tutored him in his early life. He was also a great admirer of Cato. Many of Seneca's personal letters and writings survived after his death and have been a great source of knowledge on Stoicism. Seneca's writings had great influence on some notable people, including Erasmus, Pascal, Francis Bacon and Montaigne.

With that out of the way, let's dive into the most important beliefs and principles of Stoic philosophy.

***

This is the end of this bonus chapter from **'STOICISM FOR BEGINNERS**: *Master the Art of Happiness. Learn Modern, Practical Stoicism to Create Your Own Daily Stoic Routine.'*

Want to continue reading?

Then go to Amazon and search for "Stoicism For Beginners."

Hope to see you there!

Did You Like This Book?

If you enjoyed this book, I would like to ask you for a favor. Would you be kind enough to share your thoughts and post a review of this book? Just a few sentences would already be really helpful.

Your voice is important for this book to reach as many people as possible.

The more reviews this book gets, the more people will be able to find it and learn how they, too, can benefit from applying accelerated learning tools in their lives.

***

IF YOU DID NOT LIKE THIS BOOK, THEN PLEASE TELL ME! You can email me at

feedback@semsoli.com, to share with me what you did not like.

Perhaps I can change it.

A book does not have to be stagnant, in today's world. With feedback from readers like yourself, I can improve the book. So you can impact the quality of this book, and I welcome your feedback. Help make this book better for everyone!

Thank you again for reading this book and good luck with applying everything you have learned!

I'm rooting for you...

By The Same Author

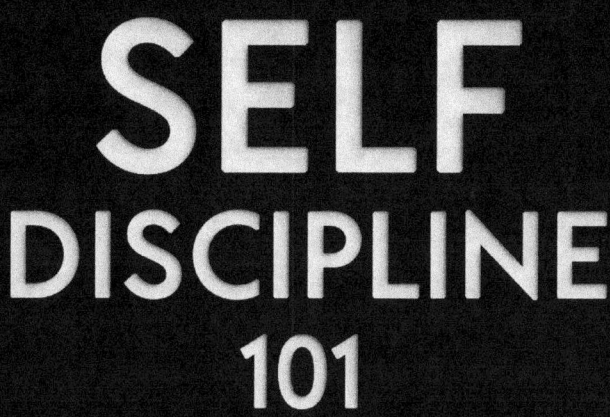

DECLUTTER YOUR LIFE

The Art of Tidying Up, Organizing Your Home, Decluttering Your Mind, & Minimalist Living (Less is More!)

KEVIN GARNETT

Minimalism 101

How Minimalist Living Can Help You To Declutter, Tidy Up Your Stuff and Say Goodbye to Things You Don't Need.

Kevin Garnett

www.ingramcontent.com/pod-product-compliance
Lightning Source LLC
Chambersburg PA
CBHW072038110526
44592CB00012B/1463